C000140922

PUPIL TEXTBOOK 1B

Noogol

Googol

Koogol

Ooogol

Toogol

Zoogol

Consultant and author
Dr Fong Ho Kheong

Authors
Chelvi Ramakrishnan and Bernice Lau Pui Wah

UK consultants
Carole Skinner, Simon d'Angelo and Elizabeth Gibbs

Introduction

Inspire Maths is a comprehensive, activity-based programme designed to provide pupils with a firm foundation in maths and to develop the creative and critical thinking skills to become fluent problem solvers.

Inspire Maths makes learning maths fun and rewarding through the use of engaging illustrations and games that help to reinforce and consolidate learning.

For the teacher:

Use the engaging and highly scaffolded **Let's Learn!** to introduce concepts. Integrated questions allow for immediate assessment and consolidation of concepts learnt.

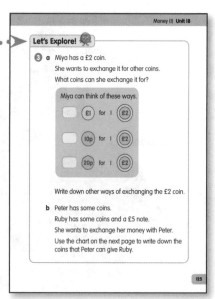

Carry out investigative activities in **Let's Explore!** These allow pupils to apply concepts learnt.

Challenge pupils to solve non-routine questions by applying relevant heuristics and thinking skills in **Put On Your Thinking Caps!**

For the parent/guardian:

Build home-school links and make maths come alive by using the tips in Home Maths to help children apply mathematical concepts to daily life.

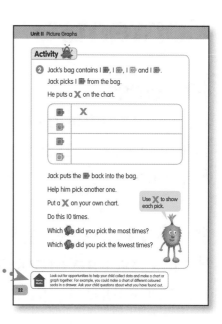

For the pupil:

Enjoy **Inspire Maths** with your friends. Explore your learning through activities and games.

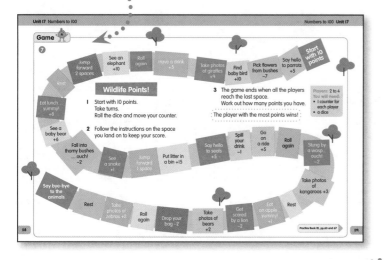

Share what you have learnt, create your own questions and become aware of your own mathematical thinking in your Maths Journal.

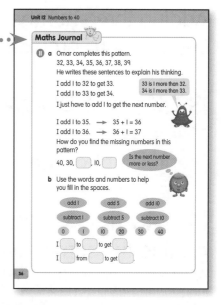

Contents

Unit 10 Mass

Let's Learn!

Comparing things

1

lion

hippo

This lion is **heavy**.

This hippo is **heavier**.

2

toy car

feather

This toy car is **light**.

This feather is **lighter**.

3 apple   orange

The apple is **as heavy as** the orange.

4

marble   ball

Which is heavier?

Which is lighter?

The ⬚ is heavier.

The ⬚ is lighter.

5

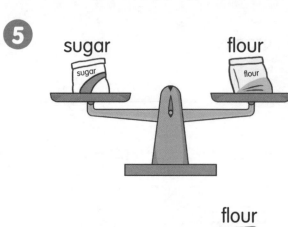

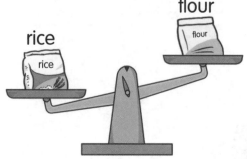

The bag of ⬚ is as heavy as the bag of ⬚.

The bag of ⬚ is the heaviest.

6

table   book   balloon

The ⬚ is the heaviest.

The ⬚ is the lightest.

Activity

7 Guess which is heavier in each set.

Use a pan balance to check your answers.

a
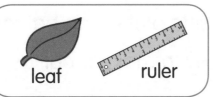
leaf   ruler

b

rubber   pencil

c
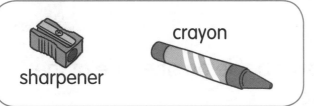
sharpener   crayon

	My guess	It is
a		a
b		b
c		c

Activity

8 You will need a pan balance, a ruler, an empty plastic bottle and some modelling clay.

1 Put the ruler on one side of the pan balance.

Use the modelling clay to make a ball as heavy as the ruler.

Name it Ball A.

2 Put the plastic bottle on one side of the pan balance.

Use the modelling clay to make another ball as heavy as the plastic bottle.

Name it Ball B.

3 Answer these questions.

a Which ball is heavier, A or B?

b Which is heavier, the ruler or the bottle?

Practice Book IC, p.5

Let's Learn!

Finding the masses of things

The mug is as heavy as 10 marbles.

The mass of the mug is 10 marbles.

2

a The mass of Bag A is ☐ marbles.

b Bag B is as heavy as ☐ marbles.

c Which is the lightest bag? ☐

d Which is the heaviest bag? ☐

e Bag ☐ is heavier than Bag ☐.

f Bag ☐ is lighter than Bag ☐.

Activity

3 **a** Use marbles and a pan balance to find the masses of these objects.

an apple   a sock   a pencil case

b Guess the mystery object.

You will need a box of objects.
Pick one object.
Find its mass using marbles.
Write its mass on a card.

My mystery object has a mass of 10 marbles.

Show some friends the box of objects and the card.
Ask them to guess what your mystery object is.
They can use marbles and a pan balance to check their guesses.

Practice Book IC, p.11

Let's Explore!

4 Work in pairs.
You will need a pan balance and three different objects.
Use the pan balance to arrange the objects in order.
Begin with the heaviest object.

Let's Learn!

Finding mass in units

1  stands for 1 unit.

The mass of the apple is about 4 units.

2 stands for 1 unit.

The mass of the same apple is about [   ] units.

Why is the number of units different?

Activity

3 Set I

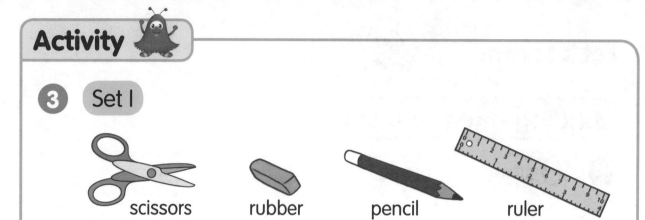

scissors   rubber   pencil   ruler

Use 📎 as I unit.

First guess the mass of each object.

Then check your answer with a pan balance.

Object	Our guess	It is
Scissors	☐ units	☐ units
Rubber	☐ units	☐ units
Pencil	☐ units	☐ units
Ruler	☐ units	☐ units

Activity

Set 2

pencil case   water bottle   box of pencils

Use 🔵 as I unit.

First guess the mass of each object.

Then check your answer using a pan balance.

Object	Our guess	It is
Pencil case	____ units	____ units
Water bottle	____ units	____ units
Box of pencils	____ units	____ units

Next use 📎 as I unit to find the masses of the objects in Set 2. Are the answers the same?

Then use 🔵 to find the masses of the objects in Set I. Are the answers the same? Can you say why?

4 stands for I unit.

orange

rubber

book

a What is the mass of the orange? ☐ units

b What is the mass of the rubber? ☐ units

c What is the mass of the book? ☐ units

d Which is the heaviest? ☐

e Which is the lightest? ☐

f Arrange the objects in order.
Begin with the heaviest.

heaviest

Practice Book IC, p.15

Put On Your Thinking Caps!

 a

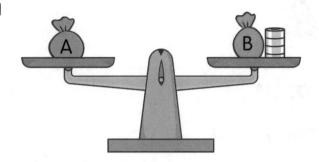

Which bag is heavier, A or B?

b

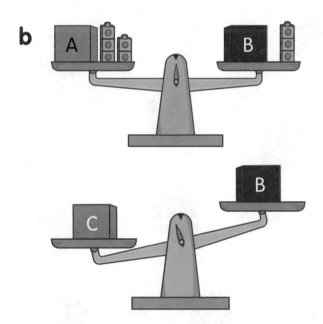

Arrange the boxes in order.
Begin with the lightest.

Practice Book IC, p.19   Practice Book IC, p.21

Picture Graphs

Let's Learn!

Simple picture graphs

Collecting and organising data

1 Sally loves stickers!
Count the number of stickers she has.

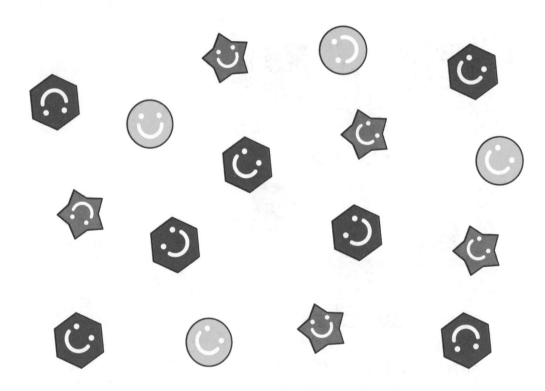

We can show the number of stickers in this way too.

Sally's Stickers

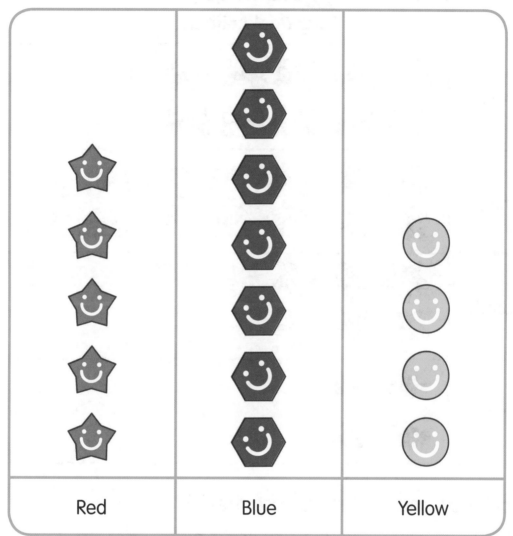

| Red | Blue | Yellow |

There are 5 red stickers.

There are 7 blue stickers.

There are 4 yellow stickers.

There are 2 more blue stickers than red stickers.

There are 3 fewer yellow stickers than blue stickers.

Altogether there are 16 stickers.

Interpreting data

2 These animals live in a rock pool.

Rock Pool Animals

Crab	
Shrimp	
Starfish	
Fish	

a How many shrimps are there?

b How many starfish are there?

c How many fish are there?

d How many crabs are there?

e Are there more shrimps or fish?
How many more?

f Are there fewer starfish or crabs?
How many fewer?

Practice Book IC, p.23

Let's Learn!

More picture graphs

Collecting and organising data

1 Ella rolls a dice.

Each ⭐ stands for 1 roll.

Ella's Rolls

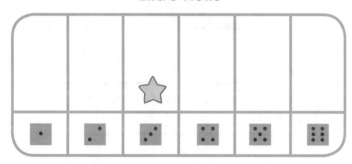

Ella rolls the dice again.

Ella's Rolls

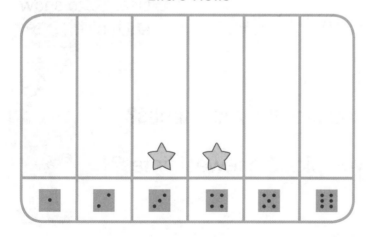

Look at what I got!

Help Ella roll the dice 10 more times.

Show the dice rolls on your own graph.

Activity

2 Jack's bag contains I ⬛, I ⬛, I ⬛ and I ⬛.

Jack picks I ⬛ from the bag.

He puts a **X** on the chart.

Jack puts the ⬛ back into the bag.

Help him pick another one.

Put a **X** on your own chart.

Use **X** to show each pick.

Do this 10 times.

Which ⬛ did you pick the most times?

Which ⬛ did you pick the fewest times?

Interpreting data

3 This graph shows the favourite toys of 20 children.

Children's Favourite Toys

Each ☆ stands for I child.

4 children like cooking sets.

3 children like dolls.

2 more children like balls than toy robots.

3 fewer children like toy cars than cooking sets.

The same number of children like balls and cooking sets.

There are 6 types of toys altogether.

The most popular toy is the teddy bear.

④ The graph shows the types of jelly beans that children like.

Types of Jelly Beans

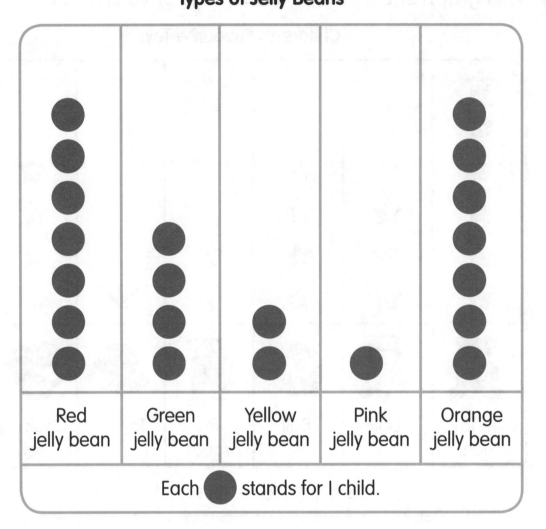

How many children like orange jelly beans?

Which jelly beans do the fewest children like?

How many more children like red jelly beans than green jelly beans?

How many fewer children like yellow jelly beans than orange jelly beans?

How many types of jelly beans are there?

Practice Book IC, p.27

Put On Your Thinking Caps!

5 Read the sentences.

Copy the graph. Fill it in.

It rains on Monday and Tuesday.

It is sunny on Wednesday and Thursday.

There is rain on Friday.

It is hot and does not rain on Saturday and Sunday.

Use ▲ to stand for I day.

Sunny Days and Rainy Days

Are there more sunny days or rainy days?

How many more?

Practice Book IC, p.34

Unit 12 Numbers to 40

Let's Learn!

Counting to 40

1 Count the .

1, 2, 3, 4, 5, 6, 7, 8, 9, 10

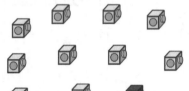

... 11, 12, 13, 14, 15, 16, 17, 18, 19, 20, 21

2 Make tens with the 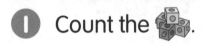 and count.

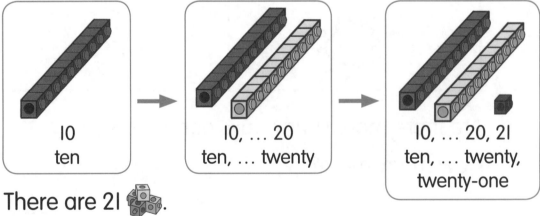

10
ten

10, ... 20
ten, ... twenty

10, ... 20, 21
ten, ... twenty, twenty-one

There are 21 .

3

Ten, ... twenty, ... thirty, thirty-one, thirty-two, thirty-three, thirty-four, thirty-five

30   31,   32,   33,   34,   35

There are 35 🔲.

4 Count in tens and ones.
What are the numbers and words?

Cubes		Numbers	Words
2 tens	4 ones		
2 tens	7 ones		
2 tens	9 ones		
3 tens	5 ones		
3 tens	8 ones		

5

40
forty

I have 40 🔲.

6

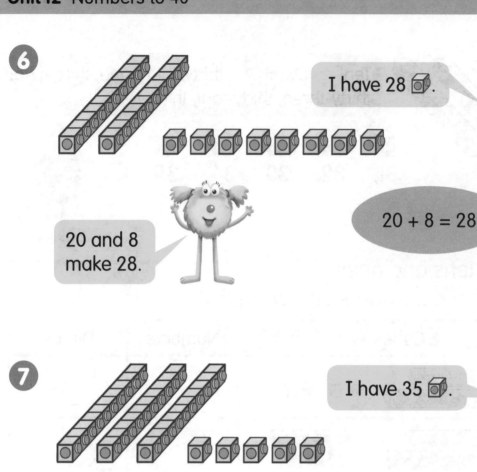

I have 28 🎲.

20 and 8 make 28.

20 + 8 = 28

7

I have 35 🎲.

30 and 5 make 35.

30 + 5 = 35

8 Find the missing number.

a 20 and 6 make ⬚.　**b** 20 and 3 make ⬚.

c 20 + 8 = ⬚　**d** 7 and 30 make ⬚.

e 9 and 30 make ⬚.　**f** 4 + 30 = ⬚

Practice Book IC, p.37

Let's Learn!

Place value

1

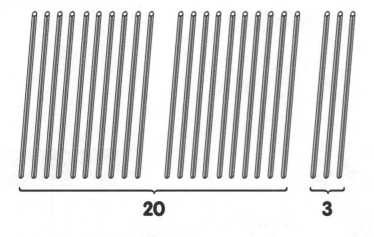

20   3

Tens	Ones
2	3

23 = 2 tens 3 ones

23 = 20 + 3

2

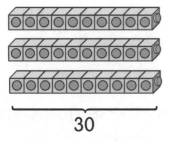   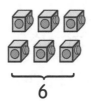

30   6

Tens	Ones
3	6

36 = 3 tens 6 ones

36 = 30 + 6

3 Find the missing numbers.

a

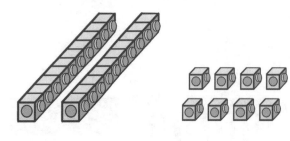

Tens	Ones

28 = ⬭ tens ⬭ ones

b

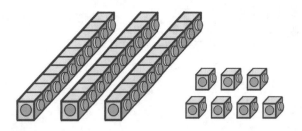

Tens	Ones

37 = ⬭ tens ⬭ ones

Activity

4 You will need 40 straws.

Put them in tens and ones to show these numbers.

(22) (27) (30) (33) (34) (35)

Practice Book IC, p.41

Let's Learn!

Comparing, order and pattern

1 This is a number track.

2 more

2 less

| 26 | 27 | 28 | 29 | 30 | 31 | 32 | 33 | 34 | 35 | 36 | 37 | 38 | 39 | 40 |

Count on from 27.

Count back from 38.

29 is 2 more than 27.

29 is greater than 27.

36 is 2 less than 38.

36 is smaller than 38.

2 This picture shows part of a calendar.

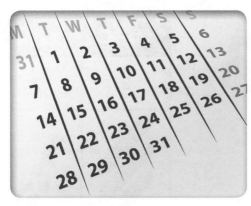

31	1	2	3	4	5	6
7	8	9	10	11	12	13
14	15	16	17	18	19	20
21	22	23	24	25	26	27
28	29	30	31			

☐ is 2 more than 22.

☐ is greater than 22.

☐ is 3 less than 31.

☐ is smaller than 31.

3 Compare 28 and 31.

The tens are different.

Compare the tens. 3 tens is greater than 2 tens.

Tens	Ones
2	8

28

Tens	Ones
3	1

31

31 is greater than 28.

4 Compare 34 and 37.

The tens are equal. We compare the ones.

7 is greater than 4.

Tens	Ones
3	4

34

Tens	Ones
3	7

37

37 is greater than 34.

5 Which number is greater?
Which number is smaller?

26   32

Are the tens equal?

☐ tens is greater than ☐ tens.

☐ is greater than ☐.

☐ is smaller than ☐.

6 Which number is greater?
Which number is smaller?

35   34

Are the tens equal?
Are the ones equal?

☐ ones is greater than ☐ ones.

☐ is greater than ☐.

☐ is smaller than ☐.

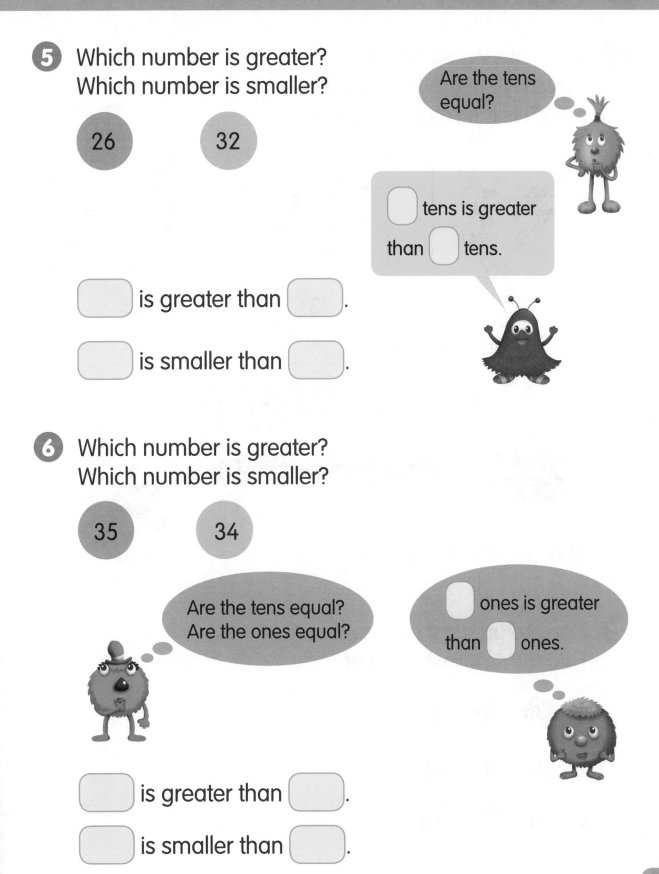

7 Compare 27, 33 and 35.
Which is the greatest number?
Which is the smallest number?

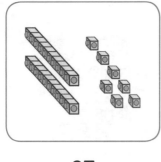   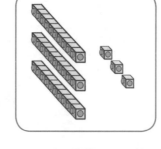   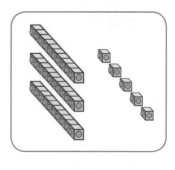

27   33   35

The smallest number is ⬚ .

Why is it the smallest number?

Why is 35 greater than 33?

The greatest number is ⬚ .

8 Find the greatest number.
Find the smallest number.

a (35) (34) (38)

b (27) (36) (30)

c (9) (18) (40)

9 The numbers on this number track are arranged in a pattern.
Some numbers are missing.

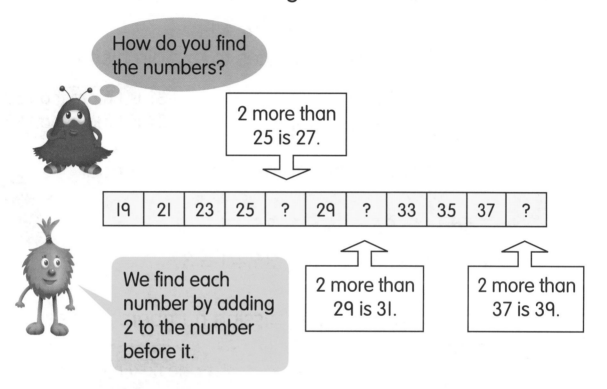

How do you find the numbers?

2 more than 25 is 27.

| 19 | 21 | 23 | 25 | ? | 29 | ? | 33 | 35 | 37 | ? |

We find each number by adding 2 to the number before it.

2 more than 29 is 31.

2 more than 37 is 39.

10 The numbers below are arranged in a pattern.
Find the missing numbers.

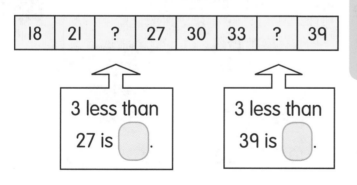

| 18 | 21 | ? | 27 | 30 | 33 | ? | 39 |

We find each number by subtracting ⬭ from the number after it.

3 less than 27 is ⬭.

3 less than 39 is ⬭.

Practice Book IC, p.45

Maths Journal

11 **a** Omar completes this pattern.

32, 33, 34, 35, 36, 37, 38, 39

He writes these sentences to explain his thinking.

I add 1 to 32 to get 33.
I add 1 to 33 to get 34.

33 is 1 more than 32.
34 is 1 more than 33.

I just have to add 1 to get the next number.

I add 1 to 35. ➝ 35 + 1 = 36
I add 1 to 36. ➝ 36 + 1 = 37

How do you find the missing numbers in this pattern?

40, 30, ☐, 10, ☐

Is the next number more or less?

b Use the words and numbers to help you fill in the spaces.

add 1   add 5   add 10

subtract 1   subtract 5   subtract 10

0   1   10   20   30   40

I ☐ to ☐ to get ☐.

I ☐ from ☐ to get ☐.

Let's Learn!

Simple addition

1 24 + 3 = ?

There are different ways to get the answer.

a Count on from 24.

24	25	26	27

24, **25, 26, 27**

b Use a place value chart.

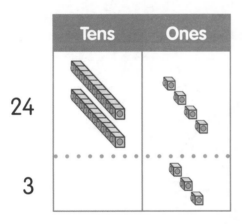

First add the ones.

Tens   Ones

  2   **4**
+   **3**
_____
        7

4 ones + 3 ones = 7 ones

Then add the tens.

Tens   Ones

  2   4
+   3
_____
  2   7

2 tens + 0 tens = 2 tens

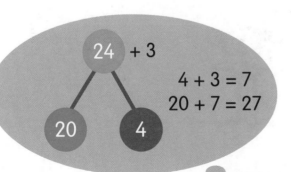

24 + 3

4 + 3 = 7
20 + 7 = 27

20   4

24 + 3 = 27

2 36 + 2 = ?

a Count on from 36.

36, ☐ , ☐

b Use a place value chart.

Tens	Ones
36	
2	

First add the ones.
Then add the tens.

```
     Tens  Ones
        3    6
   +         2
   _____
   ┌─────────┐
   └─────────┘
```

36 + 2

30   ?

☐ + 2 = ☐

30 + ☐ = ☐

36 + 2 = ☐

3 17 + 20 = ?

a Count on from 20.

20, ...**30**, ...**37**

b Use a place value chart.

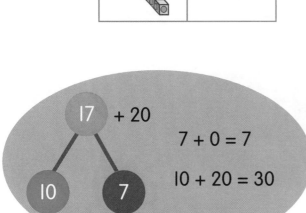

Tens	Ones
17	
20	

First add the ones.

Tens	Ones
1	7
+ 2	0
	7

7 ones + 0 ones = 7 ones

Then add the tens.

Tens	Ones
1	7
+ 2	0
3	7

1 ten + 2 tens = 3 tens

17 + 20

10   7

7 + 0 = 7

10 + 20 = 30

17 + 20 = 37

39

4 20 + 10 = ?

a Count on from 20.

20, ... ⬚

b Use a place value chart.

First add the ones.
Then add the tens.

Tens	Ones

20

10

Tens Ones

$$\begin{array}{cc} 2 & 0 \\ + 1 & 0 \\ \hline \end{array}$$

⬚

2 tens + 1 ten = ⬚ tens

20 + 10 = ⬚

20 + 10 = ⬚

5 25 + 10 = ⬚

6 18 + 30 = ⬚

7 14 + 25 = ?

Use a place value chart.

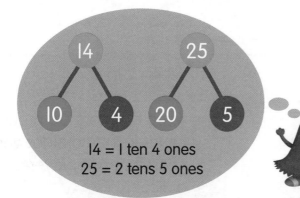

14 = 1 ten 4 ones
25 = 2 tens 5 ones

	Tens	Ones
14		
25		

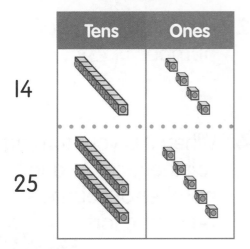

First add the ones.

Tens	Ones
1	4
+ 2	5
	9

4 ones + 5 ones = 9 ones

Then add the tens.

Tens	Ones
1	4
+ 2	5
3	9

1 ten + 2 tens = 3 tens

14 + 25 = 39

8 22 + 16 = ⬜

Practice Book IC, p.51

41

Let's Learn!

More addition

Game

① **Race to 40!**

How to play:

Players: 2 to 4
You will need:
- 4 red counters, 20 green counters and a place value chart for each player
- a dice

1 Red counters stand for tens. Green counters stand for ones.

2 Roll the dice to get a number.

3 Put this number of green counters on your chart. The other players take turns to roll the dice.

4 When it is your turn again, roll the dice. Add to the number of counters on your chart.

5 If you get 10 green counters, swap them for 1 red counter.

The first player to get 4 red counters or 4 tens wins!

② Regroup the ones into tens and ones.
Use counters to help you.

Tens	Ones		Tens	Ones
1	14	=		4

3 28 + 6 = ?
Use a place value chart.

28 = 2 tens 8 ones

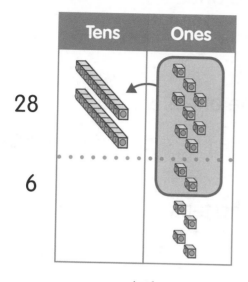

28

6

First add the ones.

Tens	Ones
2	8
+	6
	4
1	

8 ones + 6 ones = 14 ones

Regroup the ones.

14 ones = 1 ten 4 ones

Then add the tens.

Tens	Ones
2	8
+	6
3	4
1	

2 tens + 1 ten = 3 tens

34

28 + 6 = 34

Home Maths
Explain to your child that in the question above, 8 ones are added to 6 ones, which makes 14 ones altogether. 14 ones is the same as 1 ten and 4 ones. The tens need to be carried over to the tens column, so we write a small 1 in the tens column to show this.

4 Add the numbers.

a

Tens	Ones
1	2
+	8

First add the ones.

[ ] ones + [ ] ones = [ ] ones

Regroup the ones.

[ ] ones = [ ] ten [ ] ones

Then add the tens.

[ ] ten + [ ] ten = [ ] tens

b

3	1
+	9

c

2	5
+	7

d

2	9
+	6

e

3	5
+	8

5 14 + 18 = ?

Use a place value chart.

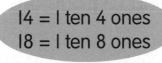
14 = 1 ten 4 ones
18 = 1 ten 8 ones

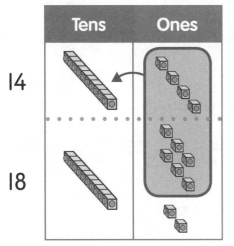

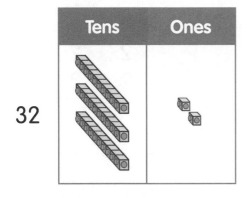

First add the ones.

Tens   Ones

	Tens	Ones
	1	4
+	1	8
		2

4 ones + 8 ones = 12 ones

Regroup the ones.

12 ones = 1 ten 2 ones

Then add the tens.

Tens   Ones

	Tens	Ones
	1	4
+	1	8
	3	2

1 ten + 1 ten + 1 ten = 3 tens

14 + 18 = 32

6 Add and regroup the numbers.

a   Tens Ones

      | 5
  + | 6
  _____

First add the ones.

[   ] ones + [   ] ones = [   ] ones

Regroup the ones.

[   ] ones = [   ] ten [   ] one

Then add the tens.

[   ] ten + [   ] ten + [   ] ten

= [   ] tens

b | 5
  + | 5
  _____

c   2   2
  +   2   8
  _____

d | 2
  + | 9
  _____

e | 7
  + | 7
  _____

Practice Book IC, p.55

Let's Learn!

Simple subtraction

There are different ways to get the answer.

1 27 − 4 = ?

a Count back from 27.

27, **26**, **25**, **24**, **23**

b Use a place value chart.

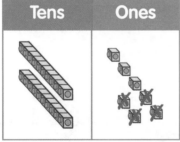

27

Tens	Ones

First subtract the ones.

Tens	Ones
2	7
−	4
	3

7 ones − 4 ones = 3 ones

23

Tens	Ones

Then subtract the tens.

Tens	Ones
2	7
−	4
2	3

2 tens − 0 tens = 2 tens

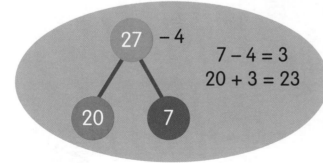

27 − 4

20   7

7 − 4 = 3
20 + 3 = 23

27 − 4 = 23

2 36 − 3 = ?

a Count back from 36.

36, ⬜, ⬜, ⬜

b Use a place value chart.

Tens	Ones
36 (3 tens rods)	(6 ones cubes)

Tens	Ones		Tens	Ones
⬜ (3 tens rods)	(ones cubes, 3 crossed out)		3	6
		−		3
			⬜	

First subtract the ones.
Then subtract the tens.

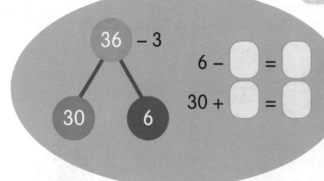

36 − 3

30   6

6 − ⬜ = ⬜

30 + ⬜ = ⬜

36 − 3 = ⬜

3 30 – 20 = ?

a Count back from 30.

30, ... ⬜ , ... ⬜

b Use a place value chart.

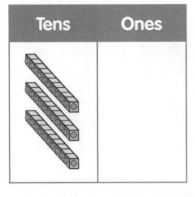

Tens	Ones

30

First subtract the ones.
Then subtract the tens.

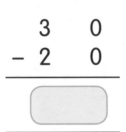

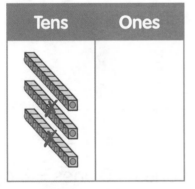

Tens	Ones

10

Tens Ones

$$\begin{array}{cc} 3 & 0 \\ -\ 2 & 0 \\ \hline \ \ \boxed{} & \\ \hline \end{array}$$

3 tens – 2 tens = ⬜ ten

30 – 20 = ⬜

30 – 20 = ⬜

4 38 − 20 = ?

Use a place value chart.

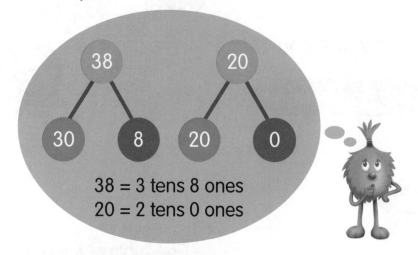

38 = 3 tens 8 ones
20 = 2 tens 0 ones

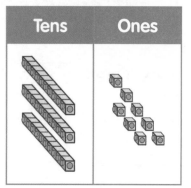

38

First subtract the ones.

	Tens	Ones
	3	8
−	2	0
		8

8 ones − 0 ones = 8 ones

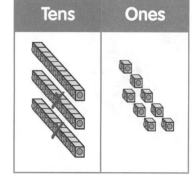

18

Then subtract the tens.

	Tens	Ones
	3	8
−	2	0
	1	8

3 tens − 2 tens = 1 ten

38 − 20 = 18

5 39 − 22 = ?

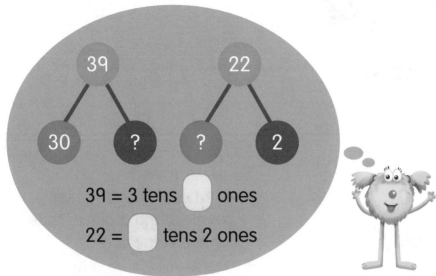

39 = 3 tens ☐ ones

22 = ☐ tens 2 ones

Tens	Ones

39

First subtract the ones.
Then subtract the tens.

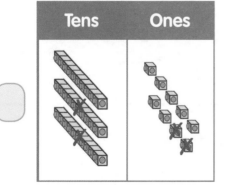

Tens Ones

```
   3  9
-  2  2
_____
```

39 − 22 = ☐

Practice Book IC, p.59

Let's Learn!

More subtraction

Game

1 **Race to 0!**

How to play:

Players: 2 to 4
You will need:
- 4 red counters, 20 green counters and a place value chart for each player
- a dice

1 Red counters stand for tens. Green counters stand for ones.

2 Put 4 red counters on your chart.

3 Swap 1 red counter for 10 green counters. Then roll the dice.

4 Take away this number of green counters from your chart. Players take turns to roll the dice and take away.

The first player to take away all the counters or get 0 wins!

2 Regroup the ones into tens and ones.
Use counters to help you.

	Tens	Ones		Tens	Ones
25 =	2	5	=	1	

3 32 − 9 = ?

First subtract the ones. We can't subtract 9 ones from 2 ones, so we regroup the tens and ones in 32.

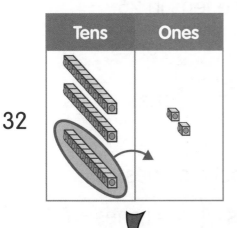

32

Regroup the tens in 32.

3 tens = 2 tens 10 ones

First subtract the ones.

Tens	Ones
²3̶	¹2
−	9
	3

12 ones − 9 ones = 3 ones

Then subtract the tens.

Tens	Ones
²3̶	¹2
−	9
2	3

2 tens − 0 tens = 2 tens

23

32 − 9 = 23

4 Subtract the numbers.

a

Tens Ones

2 6

– 7

—————

[　　]

Regroup the tens in 26.

26 = 2 tens [　　] ones

= 1 ten [　　] ones

First subtract the ones.

[　　] ones – [　　] ones = [　　] ones

Then subtract the tens.

[　　] ten – [　　] tens = [　　] ten

b

Tens Ones

2 3

– 6

—————

[　　]

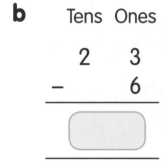

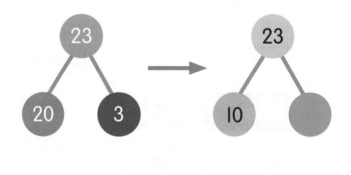

c

Tens Ones

3 2

– 8

—————

[　　]

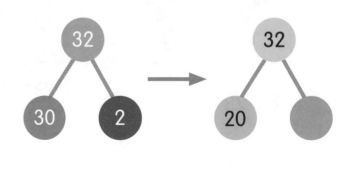

5 40 − 29 = ?

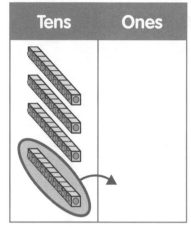

First subtract the ones. We can't subtract 9 ones from 0 ones, so we regroup the tens and ones in 40.

Regroup the tens in 40.

4 tens = 3 tens 10 ones

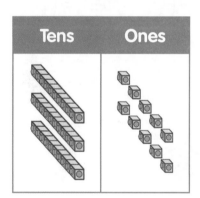

First subtract the ones.

Tens   Ones

$^3\!\!\not{4}$ $^1 0$
− 2   9

1

10 ones − 9 ones = 1 one

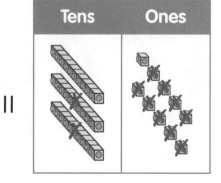

Then subtract the tens.

Tens   Ones

$^3\!\!\not{4}$ $^1 0$
− 2   9

1   1

3 tens − 2 tens = 1 ten

40 − 29 = 11

6 Regroup and subtract the numbers.

a

Tens Ones

3 4
– 1 5
⎯⎯⎯⎯
[ ]
⎯⎯⎯⎯

Regroup the tens in 34.

34 = 3 tens [ ] ones

= 2 tens [ ] ones

First subtract the ones.

[ ] ones – [ ] ones = [ ] ones

Then subtract the tens.

[ ] tens – [ ] ten = [ ] ten

b

Tens Ones

3 1
– 1 9
⎯⎯⎯⎯
[ ]
⎯⎯⎯⎯

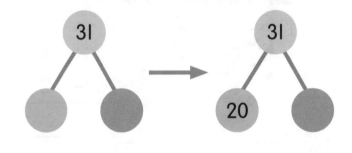

c

Tens Ones

3 5
– 2 8
⎯⎯⎯⎯
[ ]
⎯⎯⎯⎯

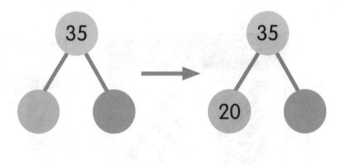

Practice Book IC, p.63

56

Let's Learn!

Adding three numbers

 5 + 7 + 6 = ?

a

5 + 7 + 6

Step 1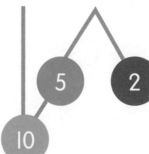

Make 10 first.
5 + 5 = 10

Step 2   2 + 6 = 8

Step 3   10 + 8 = 18

5 + 7 + 6 = 18
or

b

5 + 7 + 6

Step 1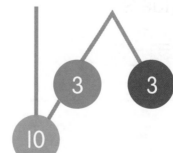

Make 10 first.
7 + 3 = 10

Step 2   5 + 3 = 8

Step 3   10 + 8 = 18

5 + 7 + 6 = 18

2 6 + 8 + 3 = ☐

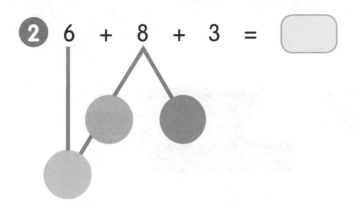

3 9 + 6 + 5 = ☐

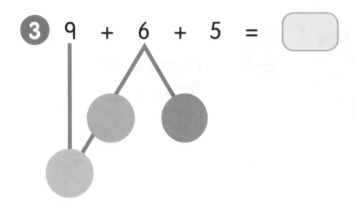

Practice Book IC, p.67

Let's Explore!

4 Show two ways to add the three numbers.

9 + 7 + 8 = ☐

Use number bonds to make tens.

Let's Learn!

Solving word problems

1 Peter has 15 .
Miya has 3 more than Peter.
How many does Miya have?

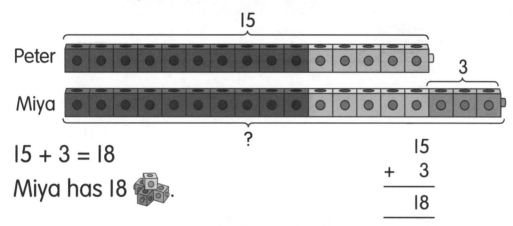

15 + 3 = 18
Miya has 18 .

$$\begin{array}{r} 15 \\ +3 \\ \hline 18 \end{array}$$

2 Liam pours 10 glasses of orange squash.
Emma pours 8 more glasses of orange squash than Liam.
How many glasses of orange squash does Emma pour?

We can use to show
the number of glasses of
orange squash.

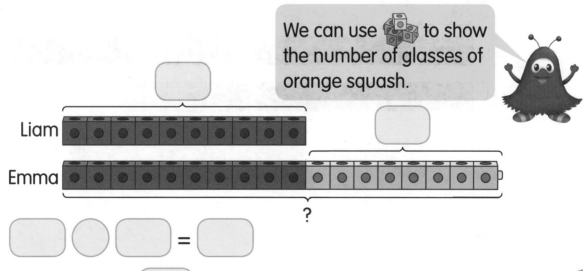

⬭ ⬭ ⬭ = ⬭

Emma pours ⬭ glasses of orange squash.

3 Hardeep lives at number 14 Green Lane.
His house number is 11 more than Ruby's.
What is Ruby's house number?

We can use 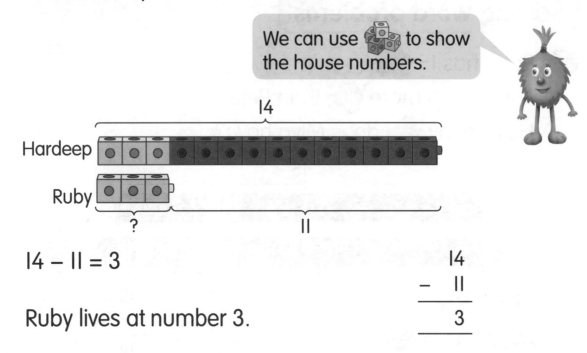 to show the house numbers.

14 − 11 = 3

$$\begin{array}{r} 14 \\ - \ 11 \\ \hline 3 \end{array}$$

Ruby lives at number 3.

4 Ben makes 20 cakes for a party.
He makes 6 more cakes than Nick.
How many cakes does Nick make?

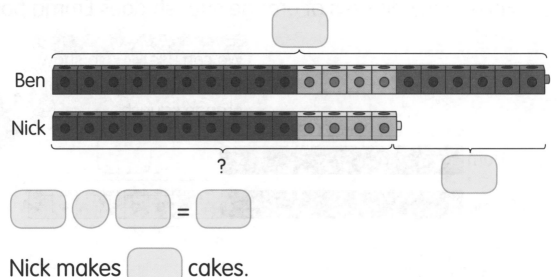

Nick makes ⬚ cakes.

5 Millie has 19 marbles.
Anna has 7 fewer marbles than Millie.
How many marbles does Anna have?

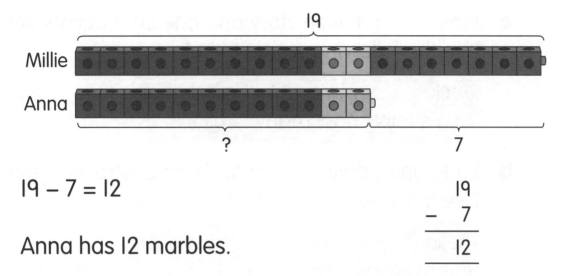

$19 - 7 = 12$

Anna has 12 marbles.

$$\begin{array}{r} 19 \\ -7 \\ \hline 12 \\ \hline \end{array}$$

6 Amy has 16 stickers.
Serge has 7 fewer stickers than Amy.
How many stickers does Serge have?

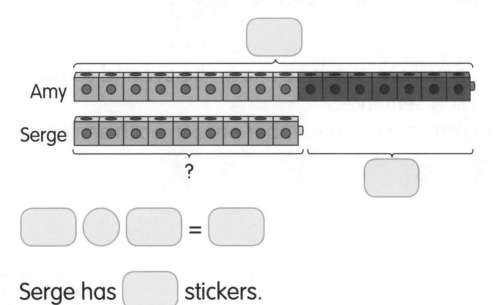

⬭ ◯ ⬭ = ⬭

Serge has ⬭ stickers.

Activity

7 Work in pairs.

a Write one addition story and one subtraction story. Use the following words to help you.

> Jack   Miya   more than
> sea shells   how many   collects

b Write one addition story and one subtraction story. Use the following words to help you.

> Bella   Tom   less than
> sandwiches   how many   makes

Practice Book IC, p.71

Put On Your Thinking Caps!

8 Pick any three numbers shown below and complete the addition sentences.
You can only use a number once in each sentence.

2   3   4   5   6   7

☐ + ☐ + ☐ = 12

☐ + ☐ + ☐ = 12

Practice Book IC, p.73

☐ + ☐ + ☐ = 12

Practice Book IC, p.74

Unit 13 — Mental Calculations

Let's Learn!

Mental addition

1 What is 12 + 6?

Regroup 12 into tens and ones.

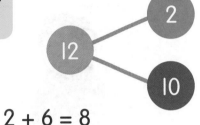

First add the ones.

$2 + 6 = 8$

Then add the result to the tens.

$10 + 8 = 18$

$12 + 6 = 18$

2 What is 15 + 20?

Regroup 15 into tens and ones.

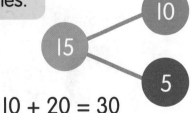

First add the tens.

$10 + 20 = 30$

Then add the result to the ones.

$5 + 30 = 35$

$15 + 20 = 35$

3 **a** $13 + 4 = \boxed{}$

b $23 + 10 = \boxed{}$

Game

4 Add mentally!

How to play:

Players: 2 to 4
You will need:
- a set of cards with numbers 4, 5, 6, 7, 8 and 9
- a set of cards with numbers 6, 7, 8 and 9

I Player I takes a card from each set.

2 Player I adds the two numbers mentally.

8 + 5 = ?

3 The other players check the answer.

8 + 5 = 13   Correct!

4 You get I point for each correct answer.
Take turns to play.

The first player to get 5 points wins!

Practice Book IC, p.81

Let's Learn!

Mental subtraction

1 What is 9 – 4?

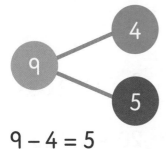

9 – 4 = 5

Think of addition.
4 and 5 make 9.

2 What is 8 – 5?

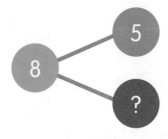

8 – 5 = ⬚

Think of addition.
5 and ⬚ make 8.

3 What is 13 – 6?

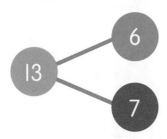

13 – 6 = 7

4 What is 15 – 9?

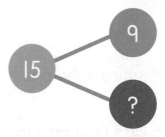

15 – 9 = ⬚

5 What is 28 − 3?

Regroup 28 into tens and ones.

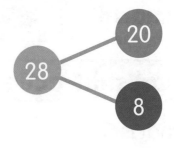

First subtract the ones.

$8 − 3 = 5$

Then add the result to the tens.

$20 + 5 = 25$

$28 − 3 = 25$

6 What is 37 − 4?

Regroup 37 into tens and ones.

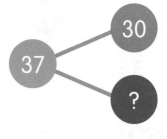

First subtract the ones.

☐ − 4 = ☐

Then add the result to the tens.

☐ + ☐ = ☐

$37 − 4 =$ ☐

7 What is 39 – 10?

Regroup 39 into tens and ones.

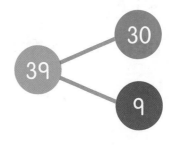

First subtract the tens.

$30 - 10 = 20$

Then add the result to the ones.

$9 + 20 = 29$

$39 - 10 = 29$

8 What is 35 – 20?

Regroup 35 into tens and ones.

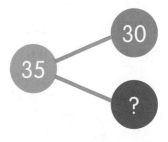

First subtract the tens.

$30 - \boxed{} = \boxed{}$

Then add the result to the ones.

$\boxed{} + \boxed{} = \boxed{}$

$35 - 20 = \boxed{}$

Game

9 **Subtract mentally!**

How to play:

Players: 2 to 4
You will need:
- a spinner with numbers 0 to 9
- a set of cards with numbers 11 to 19

1 Player 1 takes a card from the set.

2 Then they spin the spinner once to get another number.

3 Next they subtract the smaller number from the greater number.

$15 - 6 = ?$

4 The other players check the answer.
You get 1 point for each correct answer.
Take turns to play.

I win!

The first player to get 5 points wins!

Practice Book 1C, p.83

Let's Explore!

10 There are many ways to add two I-digit numbers mentally.

> **Example**
>
> 8 + 7 = ?
>
> This is one way:

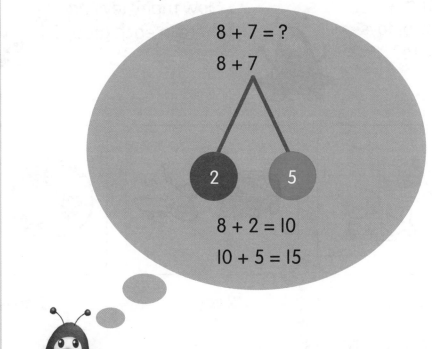

8 + 7 = ?

8 + 7

2   5

8 + 2 = 10

10 + 5 = 15

Think of another way to add 7 and 8 mentally.

Now think of two different ways to add 6 and 7.

 **14** Multiplication

Let's Learn!

Adding the same number

 How many groups of toys are there?

How many toys are there in each group?

2 toys   **2 toys**   **2 toys**

There are 3 groups.

Each group has 2 toys.

2 + 2 + 2 = 6

   3 twos = 6

3 groups of 2 = 6

There are 6 toys altogether.

2 + 2 + 2
means 3 twos or
3 groups of 2

There are ⬜ groups.

Each group has ⬜ marbles.

 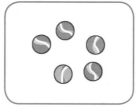

⬜ + ⬜ + ⬜ + ⬜ = ⬜

⬜ fives = ⬜

⬜ groups of 5 = ⬜

There are ⬜ marbles altogether.

3

⬜ + ⬜ + ⬜ = ⬜

⬜ fours = ⬜

⬜ groups of 4 = ⬜

There are ⬜ stars altogether.

Activity

4 How many counters are there?

a Take 5 plates.

Put 2 counters on each plate.

◻ + ◻ + ◻ + ◻ + ◻ = ◻

◻ twos = ◻

◻ groups of 2 = ◻

b Take 6 plates.

Put 3 counters on each plate.

◻ + ◻ + ◻ + ◻ + ◻ + ◻

= ◻

◻ threes = ◻

◻ groups of 3 = ◻

c Take 3 plates.

Put an equal number of counters on each plate.

◻ + ◻ + ◻ = ◻

3 ◻ = ◻

3 groups of ◻ = ◻

Practice Book IC, p.85

Let's Learn!

Making up multiplication stories

1

Ella has 5 groups of socks.
Each group has 2 socks.

$2 + 2 + 2 + 2 + 2 = 10$

5 groups of $2 = 10$

$5 \times 2 = 10$

There are 10 socks.

> **×** is read as **times**.
> It stands for **multiplication**.
> It means to put all the groups together.

$5 \times 2 = 10$ is a **multiplication sentence**.
It says **five times two equals ten**.

Tai puts his toys into 5 groups in this way.

He is trying to write a multiplication sentence.

> Can he do it?

2 Tell a multiplication story about these fish.

I see ⬚ groups of fish.

Each group has ⬚ fish.

⬚ × ⬚ = ⬚

There are ⬚ fish.

Activity

3 Tell multiplication stories about these things.
Write the multiplication sentences.

a

b

c

Practice Book IC, p.91

Maths Journal

4 Read the sentences.

Which are correct?

a $4 \times 5 = 20$

b 5×2 has the answer 52.

c The pictures show 4×4.

d $8 \times 3 = 3 + 3 + 3 + 3 + 3 + 3 + 3 + 3$

e $2 \times 6 = 6 + 6 + 6 + 6 + 6 + 6$

f $4 \times 7 = 7 + 7 + 7 + 7 = 28$

Think of some numbers.

Make multiplication sentences using these numbers.

Let's Learn!

Solving word problems

1

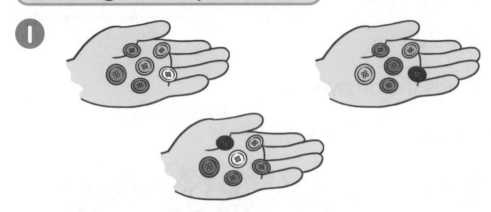

There are 3 children.

A teacher gives each child 6 buttons.

How many buttons does the teacher give out altogether?

3 × 6 = 18

The teacher gives out 18 buttons altogether.

2

Farha has 2 baskets.

There are 4 carrots in each basket.

How many carrots does Farha have altogether?

Farha has [ ] carrots altogether.

3

Peter has 5 plates.

He puts 4 cherries on each plate.

How many cherries does Peter have altogether?

 4

The plant has 6 leaves.

Ruby sees 4 ladybirds on every leaf.

How many ladybirds does Ruby see altogether?

Practice Book IC, p.95

Let's Explore!

5 **a** You have 12 balls.
Arrange them into rows in different ways.
Each row must have the same number of balls.
Write a multiplication sentence for
each arrangement.

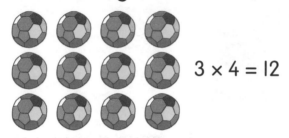 $3 \times 4 = 12$

b You have 18 balls.
Do the same as above.
How many multiplication sentences can you write?

Put On Your Thinking Caps!

6 Omar has 3 rabbits.
Which one of the following shows the number
of legs Omar's rabbits have altogether?

$3 + 3 + 3 = 9$ $3 + 3 = 6$

$3 \times 4 = 12$ $3 \times 3 = 9$

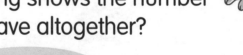

Practice Book IC, p.99   Practice Book IC, p.100

Let's Learn!

Sharing equally

1 There are 12 oranges.
Tai has 4 friends.
He gives each friend the same
number of oranges in a bag.

Jack   Millie   Ella   Omar

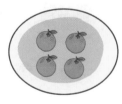

Try putting 2 oranges
in each bag. There are
4 oranges left.

Each friend gets 3 oranges.

Now put 1 more orange
in each bag. There are
no oranges left.

Activity

2 Work in pairs.

You will need 20 counters and 4 plates.

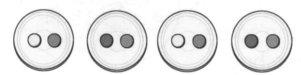

Put an equal number of counters on each plate.
Use all the counters.

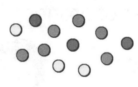

Start with a small number of counters.

How many counters are there on each plate?

 3

How many cherries are there altogether? ⬚

How many cakes are there? ⬚

Put the same number of cherries on each cake.

Each cake has ⬚ cherries.

Practice Book ID, p.5

Let's Learn!

Finding the number of groups

First put 4 eggs into 1 bowl.

1 There are 12 eggs.
Put 4 eggs into each bowl.
How many bowls do you need?

Do this until all the eggs are put into the bowls.

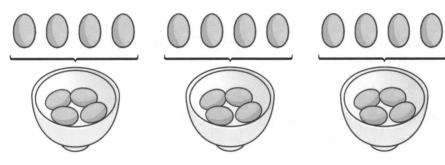

You need 3 bowls.

2 Millie has 15 toy cars.
She puts 3 toy cars on each mat.
How many mats does she need for all the toy cars?

She needs [ ] mats for all the toy cars.

Activity

3 **a** You will need 12 marbles and some cups.

Put 3 marbles in each cup.
How many cups do you need?

Put 4 marbles in each cup.
How many cups do you need?

b You will need 20 marbles and some cups.

Put 2 marbles in each cup.
How many cups do you need?

Put 4 marbles in each cup.
How many cups do you need?

Put 5 marbles in each cup.
How many cups do you need?

Put 10 marbles in each cup.
How many cups do you need?

Practice Book 1D, p.13

Let's Explore!

4 Work in pairs.

You will need 24 .

Use all the and divide them into groups.

Each group must have the same number of .

How many ways can you do it?

Maths Journal

5 Draw the different ways you can group
the in your journal.

Put On Your Thinking Caps!

6 Chris has 18 marbles.
He puts them into groups.
Each group has 5 marbles.

> Draw pictures to help you or act it out.

a What is the greatest number of groups Chris
can have?

b How many marbles are not used?

Practice Book 1D, p.19   Practice Book 1D, p.20

Time

Let's Learn!

Telling the time to the hour

 11 o'clock

 12 o'clock

1 o'clock

10 o'clock

 2 o'clock

9 o'clock

9 o'clock

— minute hand
— hour hand

 3 o'clock

8 o'clock

7 o'clock

6 o'clock

5 o'clock

 4 o'clock

When the **minute hand** is at **12**, we say it is **o'clock**.

2

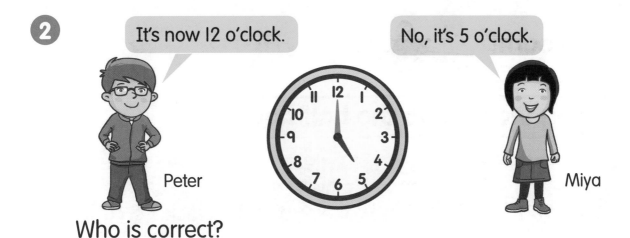

It's now 12 o'clock.

No, it's 5 o'clock.

Peter

Miya

Who is correct?

3 **a** Use a paper plate, split pin and two clock hands to make your own clock.

Then put on the numbers.

Now use your clock to show these times.

| 2 o'clock | 8 o'clock | 12 o'clock |

| 5 o'clock | 9 o'clock |

b Use the clock to show the time you do the following.

Wake up   Eat dinner   Go to bed

Eat lunch

Practice Book 1D, p.21

Let's Learn!

Telling the time to the half hour

  Millie wakes up at 7 o'clock.

Millie eats breakfast at **half past** 7.

When the **minute hand** is at **6**, we say it is **half past**.

The hour hand has moved too!

Peter feeds his cat at

in the morning.

The children play at

in the afternoon.

Ella reads a story at

at night.

Activity

5 Jack and his mum go to the fun fair.
Look at the pictures.

Work out the order the pictures should go in.

Activity

a Where are Jack and his mum at 3 o'clock?

b What time does Jack's mum win the game?

c What happens at 4 o'clock?

d Does Jack's mum buy him a balloon at half past 4?

e What do you think happens at half past 5?

Practice Book ID, p.27

Put On Your Thinking Caps!

6 **a** At half past 6, the hour hand and the minute hand are pointing to the number 6.

Is this correct?

Why?

b What time will it be when the minute hand and the hour hand are on top of each other?

Practice Book ID, p.32

Unit 17 Numbers to 100

Let's Learn!

Counting

1 Count the sticks.

10 sticks = 1 ten ten

20 sticks = 2 tens   twenty

2 Count the bundles of 10.

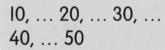
10, ... 20, ... 30, ...
40, ... 50

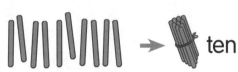

5 tens ·········· **50** ·········· fifty

6 tens ·········· **60** ·········· sixty

7 tens ·········· **70** ·········· seventy

8 tens ·················· **80** ·················· eighty

9 tens ·················· **90** ·················· ninety

10 tens ·················· **100** ·················· one hundred

3 Make tens with the and count.

Count in tens and ones.

40
forty

→

40, ... 50
forty, ... fifty

→

40, ... 50, 51, 52, 53
forty, ... fifty, fifty-one,
fifty-two, fifty-three

There are 53 .

Home Maths

Using a Snakes & Ladders board, ask your child to count from 1 to 25.
Then ask other friends or family members to continue to count the next
25 numbers until the last player reaches 100.

4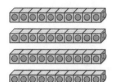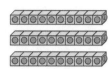

Twenty, ... thirty, ... forty, ... seventy-one, ...

20, ... 30, ... 40, ... ⬚, ... ⬚, ... ⬚

71, ⬚, ⬚, ⬚, ⬚

There are ⬚ .

5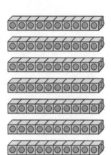

I have 74 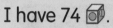.

70 + 4 = 74

70 and 4 make 74.

6 Find the missing numbers.

   a   50 + 4 = ⬚   **b**   60 and 7 make ⬚.

   c   7 and 70 make ⬚.   **d**   80 and 2 make ⬚.

   e   3 and 90 make ⬚.   **f**   9 + 90 = ⬚

Practice Book 1D, p.39

Let's Learn!

Place value

1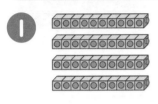

Tens	Ones
9	8

90   8

$98 = 9$ tens 8 ones

$98 = 90 + 8$

2 What are the missing numbers?

Tens	Ones
◯	◯

$87 = $ ◯ tens ◯ ones

Activity

3 You will need some straws.
Put them in tens and ones to show these numbers.

38   45   56   72   97

Practice Book ID, p.41

Let's Learn!

Comparing, order and pattern

1 You can count using this number track.

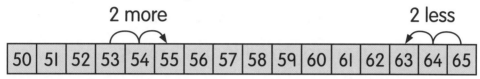

2 more

2 less

| 50 | 51 | 52 | 53 | 54 | 55 | 56 | 57 | 58 | 59 | 60 | 61 | 62 | 63 | 64 | 65 |

Count on from 53.

Count back from 65.

55 is 2 more than 53.

55 is greater than 53.

63 is 2 less than 65.

63 is smaller than 65.

2

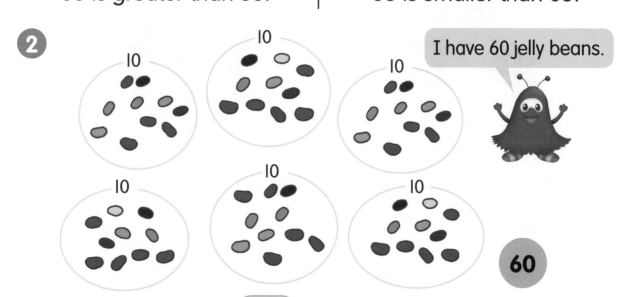

I have 60 jelly beans.

10 10 10

10 10 10

60

3 more than 60 is ☐.

3 less than 60 is ☐.

Activity

3 Work in pairs and take turns.

1 Use the two spinners.
Spin A to get a number less than 10.
Spin B to get a number less than 100.

2 Ask your partner to fill in the boxes.

☐ more than ☐ is ☐ .

☐ less than ☐ is ☐ .

Use a number track to help you.

Example

You spin the two spinners and get the following numbers.

Spinner A

Spinner B

Your partner writes the following.

3 more than **50** is **53** .

3 less than **50** is **47** .

3 less   3 more

40	41	42	43	44	45	46	47	48	49	50	51	52	53	54	55	56	57

4 Compare 60 and 59.

The tens are different.

Compare the tens. 6 tens is greater than 5 tens.

60

Tens	Ones
6	0

59

Tens	Ones
5	9

60 is greater than 59.

5 Compare 67 and 69.

The tens are the same. We compare the ones.

Compare the ones. 7 is smaller than 9.

67

Tens	Ones
6	7

69

Tens	Ones
6	9

67 is smaller than 69.

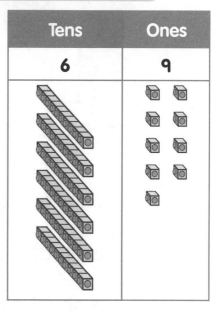

6 Which number is greater?

Which number is smaller?

Are the tens equal?

72   56

[ ] tens are greater than [ ] tens.

[ ] is greater than [ ].

[ ] is smaller than [ ].

7 Which number is greater?

Which number is smaller?

87   84

Are the tens equal?

Are the ones equal?

[ ] ones are greater than [ ] ones.

[ ] is greater than [ ].

[ ] is smaller than [ ].

8 Compare 68, 83 and 95.

Which is the smallest number?

Which is the greatest number?

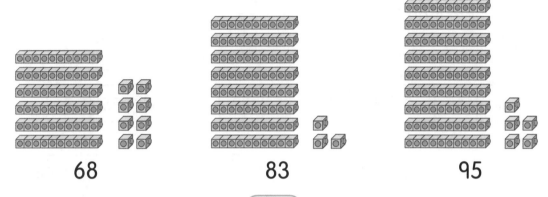

| 68 | 83 | 95 |

The smallest number is ⬚.

The greatest number is ⬚.

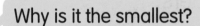

Why is it the smallest?

Why is 95 greater than 83?

9 Find the greatest number.

Find the smallest number.

a 84   48   100

b 56   59   58

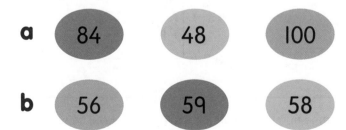

10 The numbers on this number track are arranged in a pattern.

Some numbers are missing.

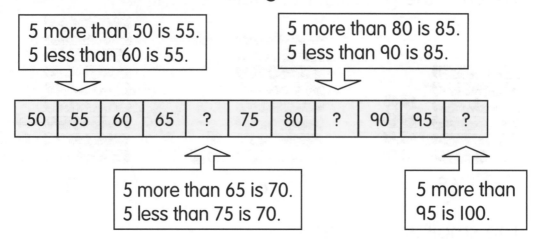

| 5 more than 50 is 55. | 5 more than 80 is 85. |
| 5 less than 60 is 55. | 5 less than 90 is 85. |

| 50 | 55 | 60 | 65 | ? | 75 | 80 | ? | 90 | 95 | ? |

5 more than 65 is 70.
5 less than 75 is 70.

5 more than 95 is 100.

11 The numbers below are arranged in a pattern.

Find the missing numbers.

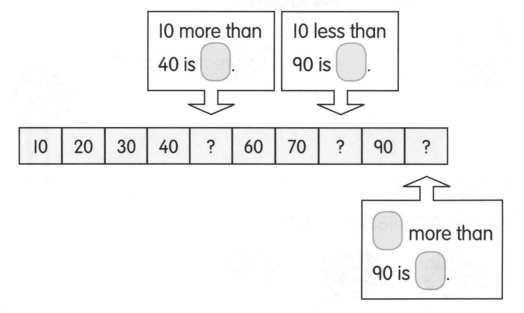

10 more than 40 is ⬚.

10 less than 90 is ⬚.

| 10 | 20 | 30 | 40 | ? | 60 | 70 | ? | 90 | ? |

⬚ more than 90 is ⬚.

Home Maths   Work with your child to make some number patterns going up by 10 each time. See if they can make a number pattern starting from 85.

Game

⑫ **What's my number?**

How to play:

1 Think of a number between 50 and 100.

2 The other players take turns to ask you questions to find the number.

3 You can answer only **Yes** or **No** to the questions.

4 See who guesses the right number first!

Practice Book ID, p.45

Let's Learn!

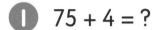 **Simple addition**

1 75 + 4 = ?

There are different ways to get the answer.

a Count on from 75.

| 75 | 76 | 77 | 78 | 79 |

75, **76, 77, 78, 79**

b Use a place value chart.

Tens	Ones

75

4

First add the ones.

Tens   Ones

7   5

+   4

          9

5 ones + 4 ones = 9 ones

Then add the tens.

Tens   Ones

7   5

+   4

7   9

7 tens + 0 tens = 7 tens

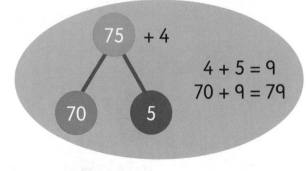

75 + 4

4 + 5 = 9
70 + 9 = 79

70   5

75 + 4 = 79

2 $82 + 5 = ?$

a Count on from 82.

82, ☐, ☐, ☐, ☐, ☐

b Use a place value chart.

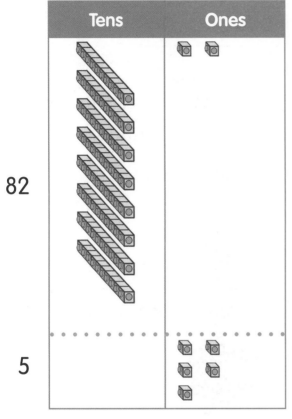

Tens	Ones
82	
5	

Tens Ones

   8   2
+   5
_____
☐

First add the ones.
Then add the tens.

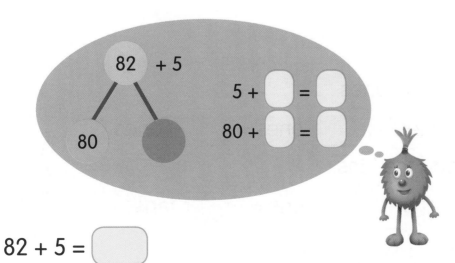

82 + 5

80

5 + ☐ = ☐
80 + ☐ = ☐

$82 + 5 = $ ☐

3 46 + 30 = ?

Use a place value chart.

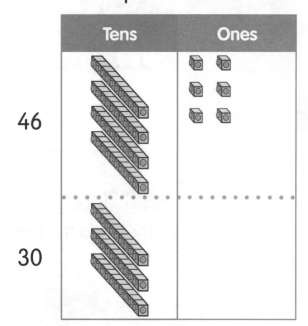

Tens	Ones

46

30

First add the ones.

Tens	Ones
4	6
+ 3	0
	6

6 ones + 0 ones = 6 ones

Then add the tens.

Tens	Ones
4	6
+ 3	0
7	6

4 tens + 3 tens = 7 tens

6 ones + 0 ones = ☐ ones

4 tens + 3 tens = ☐ tens

46 + 30 = ☐

46 + 30 = 76

4 50 + 40 = ?
First add the ones.

☐ ones + ☐ ones = ☐ ones

Then add the tens.

☐ tens + ☐ tens = ☐ tens

50 + 40 = ☐

Tens	Ones
5	0
+ 4	0
☐	

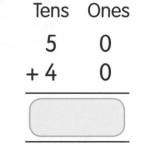

5 42 + 56 = ?

Use a place value chart.

42 = 4 tens 2 ones
56 = 5 tens 6 ones

Tens	Ones
42	
56	

42 + 56 = 98

First add the ones.

Tens   Ones
   4   2
+ 5   6
─────────
           8

2 ones + 6 ones = 8 ones

Then add the tens.

Tens   Ones
   4   2
+ 5   6
─────────
   9   8

4 tens + 5 tens = 9 tens

6 43 + 36 = ?

First add the ones.

⬭ ones + ⬭ ones = ⬭ ones

Then add the tens.

⬭ tens + ⬭ tens = ⬭ tens

43 + 36 = ⬭

Tens   Ones
   4   3
+ 3   6
─────────
    ⬭

Practice Book ID, p.49

Let's Learn!

More addition

1 66 + 7 = ?
Use a place value chart.

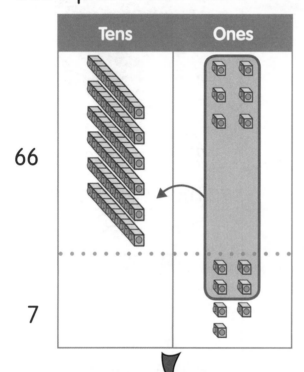

First add the ones.

Tens	Ones
6	6
+	7
	3

6 ones + 7 ones = 13 ones

Regroup the ones.

13 ones = 1 ten 3 ones

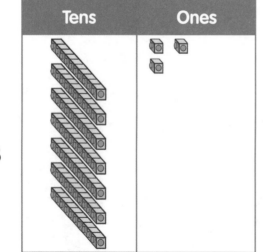

Then add the tens.

Tens	Ones
6	6
+	7
7	3

6 tens + 1 ten = 7 tens

66 + 7 = 73

2 **a** 62 + 9 = ?

First add the ones.

2 ones + 9 ones = ⬚ ones

Regroup the ones.

⬚ ones = 1 ten ⬚ one

Tens	Ones
6	2
+	9
⬚	

Then add the tens.

6 tens + ⬚ ten = ⬚ tens

62 + 9 = ⬚

b
```
    5   6
  +     8
  _____
   ⬚
  _____
```

c
```
    3   6
  +     5
  _____
   ⬚
  _____
```

d
```
    7   8
  +     5
  _____
   ⬚
  _____
```

e
```
    8   9
  +     4
  _____
   ⬚
  _____
```

Activity

Spinner

3 Work in pairs.

You will need a spinner.

1 Player 1 spins the spinner to get a number.

2 Player 1 adds this number to 52.

52 + ⬚ = ⬚

3 Player 2 spins the spinner. Player 2 adds this number to 64.

64 + ⬚ = ⬚

4 Together think of some more numbers to add to a spinner number.

4 33 + 18 = ?

33 = 3 tens 3 ones
18 = 1 ten 8 ones

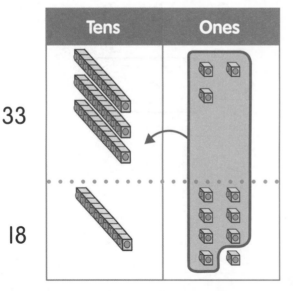

Tens	Ones
33	
18	

First add the ones.

Tens Ones

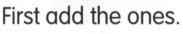

```
  Tens   Ones
    3      3
+   1      8
_____
           1
```

3 ones + 8 ones = 11 ones

Regroup the ones.

11 ones = 1 ten 1 one

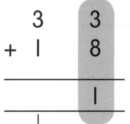

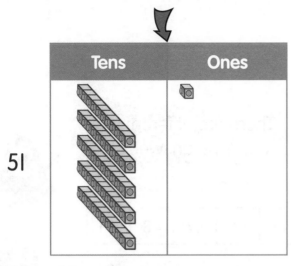

Tens	Ones

51

$33 + 18 = 51$

Then add the tens.

Tens Ones

$$
\begin{array}{cc}
3 & 3 \\
+ \ 1 & 8 \\
\hline
5 & 1 \\
\end{array}
$$

3 tens + 1 ten + 1 ten = 5 tens

5 Add and regroup the numbers.

a

Tens Ones

$$
\begin{array}{cc}
4 & 7 \\
+ \ 3 & 8 \\
\hline
\end{array}
$$

First add the ones.

◯ ones + ◯ ones = ◯ ones

Regroup the ones.

◯ ones = ◯ ten ◯ ones

Then add the tens.

◯ tens + ◯ tens + ◯ ten =

◯ tens

b

$$
\begin{array}{cc}
2 & 8 \\
+ \ 1 & 4 \\
\hline
\end{array}
$$

c

$$
\begin{array}{cc}
5 & 4 \\
+ \ 2 & 7 \\
\hline
\end{array}
$$

d

$$
\begin{array}{cc}
3 & 5 \\
+ \ 3 & 6 \\
\hline
\end{array}
$$

e

$$
\begin{array}{cc}
4 & 9 \\
+ \ 2 & 3 \\
\hline
\end{array}
$$

Practice Book ID, pp.53 and 57

Let's Learn!

Simple subtraction

There are different ways to get the answer.

① 48 – 3 = ?

40	41	42	43	44	45	46	47	48	49

a Count back from 48.

48, **47, 46, 45**

b Use a place value chart.

Tens	Ones
48	

First subtract the ones.

```
  Tens   Ones
    4      8
  −        3
  ─────────────
           5
```

8 ones – 3 ones = 5 ones

Tens	Ones
45	

Then subtract the tens.

```
  Tens   Ones
    4      8
  −        3
  ─────────────
    4      5
```

4 tens – 0 tens = 4 tens

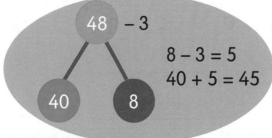

48 − 3

8 – 3 = 5
40 + 5 = 45

40   8

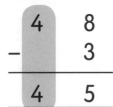

48 – 3 = 45

2 **a** $68 - 6 = \boxed{}$

b $82 - 2 = \boxed{}$

3 $70 - 40 = ?$

a Count back from 70.

b Use a place value chart.

$70, \ldots \boxed{}, \ldots \boxed{},$
$\ldots \boxed{}, \ldots \boxed{}$

Tens	Ones
70 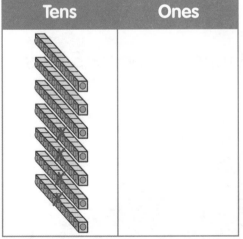	

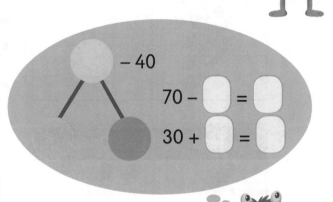

-40

$70 - \boxed{} = \boxed{}$

$30 + \boxed{} = \boxed{}$

Tens	Ones

$$\begin{array}{r} \text{Tens} \quad \text{Ones} \\ 7 \qquad 0 \\ -\ 4 \qquad 0 \\ \hline \boxed{} \\ \hline \end{array}$$

First subtract the ones.
Then subtract the tens.

$70 - 40 = \boxed{}$

4 85 − 30 = ?

Use a place value chart.

85 = 8 tens 5 ones
30 = 3 tens 0 ones

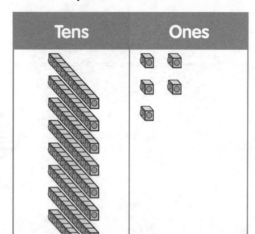

85

First subtract the ones.

Tens	Ones
8	5
− 3	0
	5

5 ones − 0 ones = 5 ones

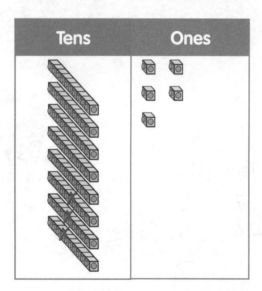

55

Then subtract the tens.

Tens	Ones
8	5
− 3	0
5	5

8 tens − 3 tens = 5 tens

85 − 30 = 55

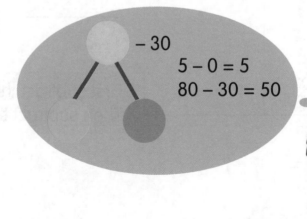

− 30

5 − 0 = 5
80 − 30 = 50

5 Subtract the numbers.

a

Tens	Ones
7	2
− 4	0

First subtract the ones.

◯ ones − ◯ ones = ◯ ones

Then subtract the tens.

◯ tens − ◯ tens = ◯ tens

b 96 − 20 = ◯

c 68 − 50 = ◯

6 58 − 24 = ?

Use a place value chart.

58 = 5 tens 8 ones
24 = 2 tens 4 ones

First subtract the ones.

Tens	Ones
5	8
− 2	4
	4

8 ones − 4 ones = 4 ones

Then subtract the tens.

Tens	Ones
5	8
− 2	4
3	4

5 tens − 2 tens = 3 tens

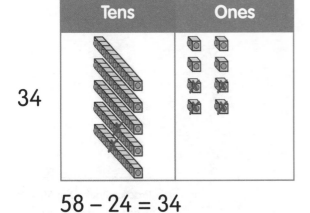

58 − 24 = 34

7 Subtract the numbers.

a

Tens	Ones
6	9
− 3	3

First subtract the ones.

[   ] ones − [   ] ones = [   ] ones

Then subtract the tens.

[   ] tens − [   ] tens = [   ] tens

b

Tens	Ones
7	5
− 2	2

First subtract the ones.

[   ] ones − [   ] ones = [   ] ones

Then subtract the tens.

[   ] tens − [   ] tens = [   ] tens

c

9	6
− 4	1

[   ]

d

8	9
− 5	7

[   ]

Practice Book ID, p.59

Let's Learn!

More subtraction

1 $52 - 9 = ?$

Tens	Ones

52

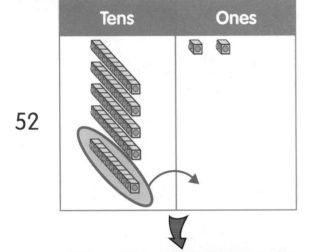

First subtract the ones.
We can't subtract
9 ones from 2 ones.
Instead we regroup the
tens and ones in 52.

Regroup the tens in 52.
52 = 5 tens 2 ones
= 4 tens 12 ones

First subtract the ones.

$$\begin{array}{cc} \text{Tens} & \text{Ones} \\ {}^4\!5 & {}^1\!2 \\ - & 9 \\ \hline & 3 \end{array}$$

12 ones – 9 ones = 3 ones

Then subtract the tens.

$$\begin{array}{cc} \text{Tens} & \text{Ones} \\ {}^4\!5 & {}^1\!2 \\ - & 9 \\ \hline 4 & 3 \end{array}$$

4 tens – 0 tens = 4 tens

Tens	Ones

43

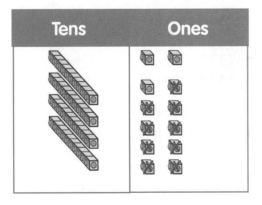

$52 - 9 = 43$

115

2 74 − 38 = ?

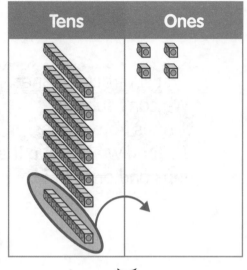

74

First subtract the ones. We can't subtract 8 ones from 4 ones. Instead we regroup the tens and ones in 74.

Regroup the tens in 74.
74 = 7 tens 4 ones
   = 6 tens 14 ones

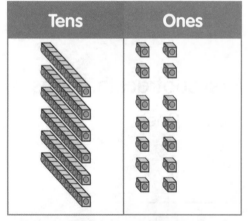

First subtract the ones.

Tens	Ones
$^6\cancel{7}$	^{14}
− 3	8
	6

14 ones − 8 ones = 6 ones

Then subtract the tens.

Tens	Ones
$^6\cancel{7}$	^{14}
− 3	8
3	6

6 tens − 3 tens = 3 tens

36

74 − 38 = 36

3 Regroup and subtract the numbers.

Tens	Ones
5	5
−	7

Regroup the tens and ones in 55.

55 = 5 tens ⬜ ones

= 4 tens ⬜ ones

First subtract the ones.

⬜ ones − ⬜ ones = ⬜ ones

Then subtract the tens.

⬜ tens − ⬜ tens = ⬜ tens

4 Subtract the numbers.

Tens	Ones
7	0
− 5	5

Regroup the tens and ones in 70.

70 = 7 tens ⬜ ones

= 6 tens ⬜ ones

First subtract the ones.

⬜ ones − ⬜ ones = ⬜ ones

Then subtract the tens.

⬜ tens − ⬜ tens = ⬜ ten

5
7	4
−	9

6
6	2
− 5	8

Game

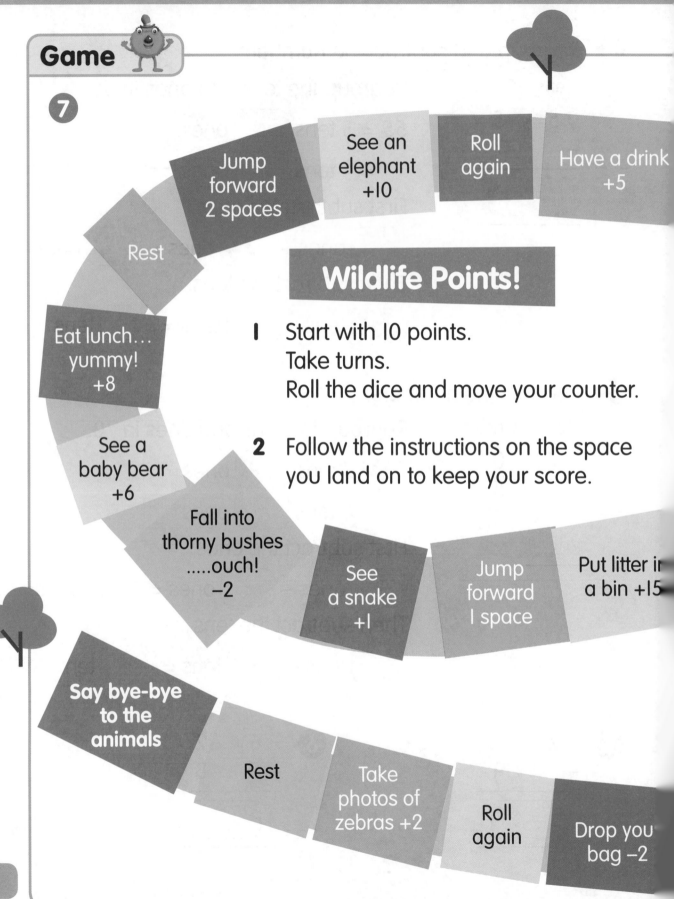

7

Jump forward 2 spaces

See an elephant +10

Roll again

Have a drink +5

Rest

Eat lunch… yummy! +8

See a baby bear +6

Fall into thorny bushes …..ouch! −2

See a snake +1

Jump forward 1 space

Put litter in a bin +15

Wildlife Points!

I Start with 10 points.
Take turns.
Roll the dice and move your counter.

2 Follow the instructions on the space you land on to keep your score.

Say bye-bye to the animals

Rest

Take photos of zebras +2

Roll again

Drop your bag −2

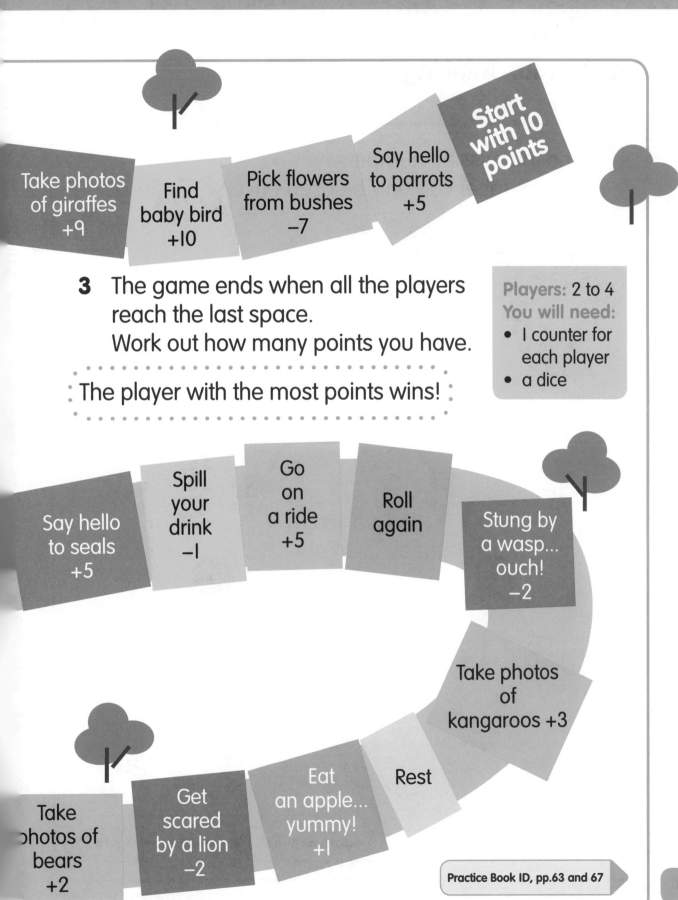

Start
with 10
points

Say hello
to parrots
+5

Pick flowers
from bushes
−7

Find
baby bird
+10

Take photos
of giraffes
+9

3 The game ends when all the players
reach the last space.
Work out how many points you have.

The player with the most points wins!

Players: 2 to 4
You will need:
• 1 counter for
each player
• a dice

Say hello
to seals
+5

Spill
your
drink
−1

Go
on
a ride
+5

Roll
again

Stung by
a wasp...
ouch!
−2

Take photos
of
kangaroos +3

Rest

Eat
an apple...
yummy!
+1

Get
scared
by a lion
−2

Take
photos of
bears
+2

Practice Book 1D, pp.63 and 67

Put On Your Thinking Caps!

8 Find the missing numbers.
Each number can only be used once.

14   25   49   39   74

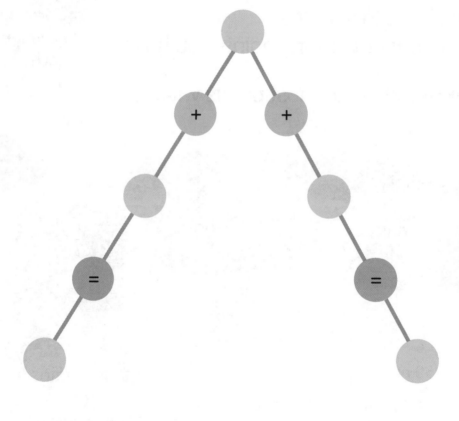

Practice Book ID, p.69   Practice Book ID, p.70

Money (1)

Let's Learn!

Getting to know our money

1

1p	2p	5p	10p	20p	50p	£1	£2
1p coin	2p coin	5p coin	10p coin	20p coin	50p coin	£1 coin	£2 coin

What can you buy with each coin?

2

£5
£5 note

£10
£10 note

£20
£20 note

£50
£50 note

> **p** means **pence!**
> **£** means **pounds!**

What can you buy with each note?

Activity

3 Count these coins and notes.

How many are there?

☐ 1p coins	☐ 2p coins	☐ 5p coins
☐ 10p coins	☐ 20p coins	☐ 50p coins
☐ £1 coins	☐ £2 coins	

How many are there?

☐ £5 notes	☐ £10 notes
☐ £20 notes	☐ £50 notes

Practice Book 1D, p.71

Let's Learn!

Exchanging money

1 We can exchange coins.

one 2p coin 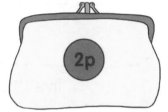 =  two 1p coins

one 5p coin  = 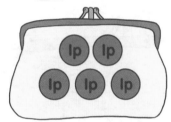 five 1p coins

one 10p coin 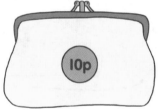 =  two 5p coins

one 20p coin 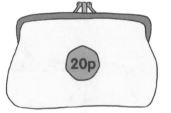 =  two 10p coins

one 50p coin 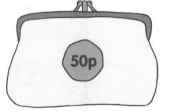 = 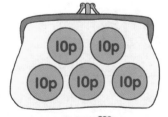 five 10p coins

one £1 coin 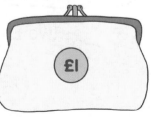 = ten 10p coins

123

2 We can also exchange coins and notes.

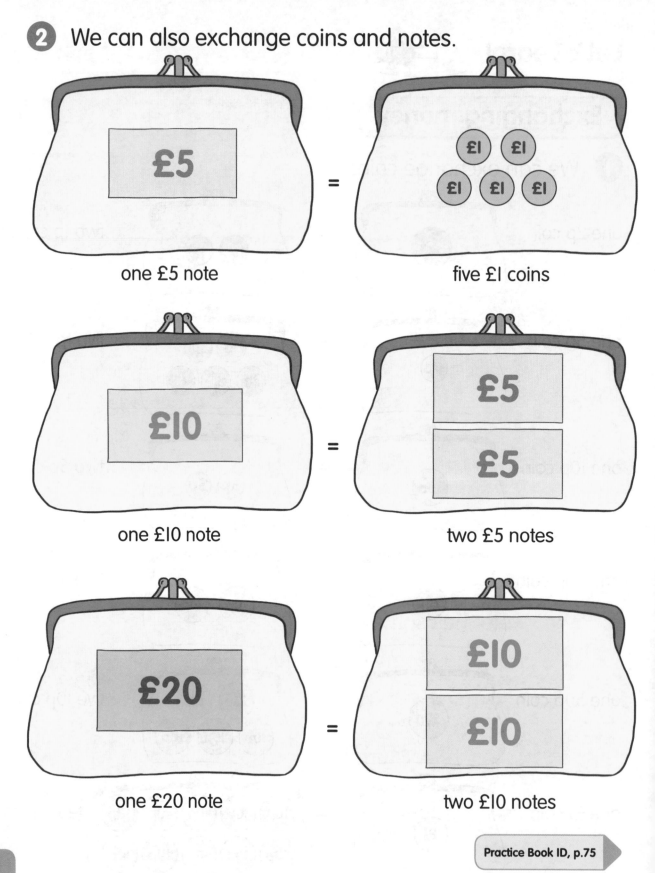

one £5 note = five £1 coins

one £10 note = two £5 notes

one £20 note = two £10 notes

Practice Book 1D, p.75

Let's Explore!

3 **a** Miya has a £2 coin.

She wants to exchange it for other coins.

What coins can she exchange it for?

Miya can think of these ways.

☐ £1 for 1 £2

☐ 10p for 1 £2

☐ 20p for 1 £2

Write down other ways of exchanging the £2 coin.

b Peter has some coins.

Ruby has some coins and a £5 note.

She wants to exchange her money with Peter.

Use the chart on the next page to write down the coins that Peter can give Ruby.

Let's Explore!

If Ruby gives Peter...	Peter can give Ruby...
2p	two 1p
10p	
20p	
£1	
£2	
£5	

c Peter has one hundred 1p coins.

He stacks them in piles of 10.

10, … 20, … 100!

10p

Peter exchanges the coins at the bank.

Use a chart to write down the coins Peter can get.

What is the fewest number of coins he can get?

Let's Learn!

Work out the amount of money

1 Count on to find how much Jack has.

50, … 70, … 80, … 85 pence

Jack has 85p.

2 Jack's mum has some money.
How much does she have?

£50

£10 £10

£10 £10

£5

50, … 60, … 70, … 80, …
90, … 95, … 97 pounds

Jack's mum has £97.

127

3 Hardeep goes shopping.

drum   apples   kite

He pays (£2) (£2) for the kite.

The kite costs £ ☐ .

He pays 5p 10p 5p 50p for the apples.

The apples cost ☐ p.

He pays   £10   £10   £10   £5   for the drum.

The drum costs £ ☐ .

4 It's lunch time and Ella is hungry.
Help her work out how to pay for different food and drinks.

I'll have a sandwich!

I'll pay with £2 and £1.

a Ella has the pizza.

She pays with ☐ .

b Ella has the apple juice.

She pays with ☐ .

Game

5 Money under my cup!

How to play:

Players: 2
You will need:
- 5p, 10p, 20p and 50p coins (three of each)
- a paper cup

1 Player 1 hides 3 coins under the cup. They must not add up to more than £1.

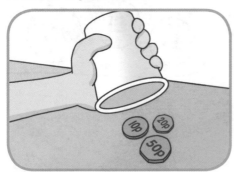

2 Player 1 says how much money is under the cup.

I have 80p.

3 Player 2 guesses which coins are hidden.

3 coins make up 80p. One 50p, one 20p and one 10p?

4 Player 1 checks the answer. Take turns to play. Have 5 turns each.

You're right!

Practice Book 1D, p.79

Maths Journal

6 | £5 | £10 | 20p 20p 50p

Which of the sentences are correct?

a There are three 20p coins.

b There is only one £5 note.

c I can exchange the coins for nine 10p coins.

d I can exchange the notes for two £1 coins.

Put On Your Thinking Caps!

7 Miya has 3 notes under a cup.

The notes add up to £50.

They can be £5, £10, £20 or £50 notes.

What are the notes under the cup?

Practice Book ID, p.85   Practice Book ID, p.87

Let's Learn!

Adding and subtracting in pence

sticker

bookmark

banana

sweets

balloon

| 60p | 30p | 50p | 35p | 65p |

1 Tai is shopping.

He has 90p.

He buys the bookmark and the sweets.

He has to pay
30p + 35p = 65p.

Ella buys a balloon.

She gives the cashier 70p.

She will get back
70p − 65p = 5p

2 You have 80p.

Which two things can you buy?

Home Maths Shopping is a good opportunity to help your child learn about money.
Ask them to look at price labels and decide which notes or coins to use.

3 Here are some things for sale.

bubbles
45p

teddy bear
70p

ball
50p

toy car
65p

toy frog
80p

toy horse
25p

a bag of marbles
30p

a bag of shells
35p

plastic flower
20p

a Abby buys a toy car and a bag of marbles.
How much does she spend?

b You have 60p to buy two things.
What can you buy?

c George buys a toy frog.
He pays with two 50p coins.
How much change does he get?

Game

4 **Roll and pay!**

Lucky dip!
Win 10p
BANK

Fine for losing
library book!
Pay 10p
BANK

Reward for
finding a
lost pet!
Get 5p
BANK

Rest

How to play:

1 Each player gets four 5p coins and
three 10p coins.
The rest of the money goes into the BANK

2 Take turns to roll the dice and move
your counter.

3 Follow the instructions on the space
you land on.

Jump
forward
3 spaces

Buy pet food!
Pay 5p
BANK

Win colouring
contest!
Get 15p BANK

Rest

End

Go back
2 spaces

Go to the park!
Pay 10p
BANK

Rest

Win game at
funfair!
Get 5p BANK

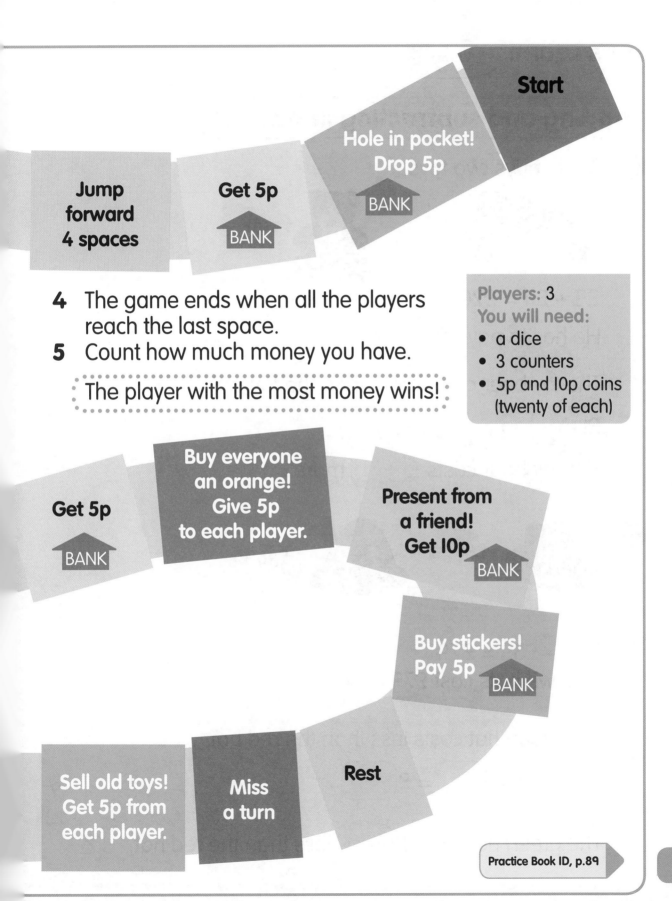

Start

Hole in pocket!
Drop 5p
BANK

Get 5p
BANK

Jump
forward
4 spaces

4 The game ends when all the players
reach the last space.
5 Count how much money you have.

The player with the most money wins!

Players: 3
You will need:
- a dice
- 3 counters
- 5p and 10p coins
  (twenty of each)

Get 5p
BANK

Buy everyone
an orange!
Give 5p
to each player.

Present from
a friend!
Get 10p
BANK

Buy stickers!
Pay 5p
BANK

Sell old toys!
Get 5p from
each player.

Miss
a turn

Rest

Practice Book 1D, p.89

Let's Learn!

Adding and subtracting in pounds

1 David buys two toys.

 £9

 £11

£9 + £11 = £20

He has to pay £20 altogether.

The toy bear costs more than the toy train.

£ ⬚ – £ ⬚ = £ ⬚

The toy bear costs £ ⬚ more.

2  £40 £39

£40 + £39 = £79
The two hats cost £79 altogether.

The green hat costs less than the red hat.

£ ⬚ – £ ⬚ = £ ⬚

The green hat costs £ ⬚ less than the red hat.

Activity

3 Set up a toy shop.

Add prices to the toys.

Use pounds only.

You have £100 to spend. What will you buy?

How much change will you get?

£12

£25

£6

£15

£32

Practice Book ID, p.97

Let's Learn!

Solving word problems

1

Stickers

85p

95p

A

B

C

60p

Toys

£8

E

£5

D

F

£7

a Jack buys all three toys.

£8 + £7 + £5 = £20

He spends £20 altogether.

b Miya buys Sticker A.

She pays with two 50p coins.

100p − 85p = 15p

She gets 15p as change.

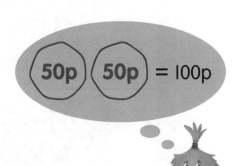

50p 50p = 100p

c Millie has 70p.

She wants to buy Sticker B.

95p − 70p = 25p

She needs 25p more.

d Peter buys toys E and F.

He has £4 left.

£7 + £5 + £4 = £16

He has £16 at first.

2

trampoline   scooter

a   Farha buys the trampoline and the scooter.
How much does she spend altogether?

£⬚ ◯ £⬚ = £⬚

Farha spends £⬚ altogether.

b   Omar buys the scooter.

He pays with £50.

How much change does Omar get?

£⬚ ◯ £⬚ = £⬚

Omar gets £⬚ change.

c   Tai buys the trampoline.
Ella buys the scooter.
How much less does Ella spend than Tai?

Ella spends £⬚ less than Tai.

d   After buying the scooter, Ruby has £8 left.
How much does Ruby have at first?

Ruby has £⬚ at first.

Practice Book ID, p.101

Let's Explore!

3 Omar, Ruby, Millie, Jack and Ella go shopping together.

These are some of the things for sale.

grapes	scooter	socks	cake
50p	£61	£6	£1

marbles	strawberries	sweets	toy spider
35p	£1	80p	20p

toy train	doll	bear	toy boat
£100	£8	£9	£5

 Home Maths Ask your child to make up some word problems about things you buy at the supermarket.

Let's Explore!

a Millie has 70p.

What two items can she buy?

b Omar has £10.

He wants to buy a toy.

After buying the toy, he will still have £5 left.

What toy does he want to buy?

c Ruby, Jack and Ella want to buy a present for Millie.

Ruby has £1, Jack has £4 and Ella has £2.

Can they buy the bear for her?

How did you find out?

d Jack has £60.

He wants to buy a toy.

Which toys cost more money than he has?

How much more money does he need for each toy?

e Ella has five 20p coins.

She wants to buy her brother two things.

Which two things can she buy?

How much does she spend on each thing?

Put On Your Thinking Caps!

4   **a** 

A pencil case costs 85p.

Miya has some 5p, 10p, 20p and 50p coins.

Show 3 ways that she can use her coins to buy the pencil case.

What is the smallest number of coins she can use to buy the pencil case?

b   Peter goes to the supermarket.

He has £40 to buy fruit for Farha, Jack and himself.

He buys two different types of fruit for each person.

What will Peter buy?

How much will he have left?

Help him to choose.

£1

£3

£5

£2

apples

bananas

apricots

melons

£1

£4

£4

£6

oranges

strawberries

blueberries

cherries

Practice Book ID, p.105

Practice Book ID, p.108

© 2015 Marshall Cavendish Education Pte Ltd

Published by Marshall Cavendish Education
Times Centre, 1 New Industrial Road, Singapore 536196
Customer Service Hotline: (65) 6213 9444
Email: tmesales@mceducation.com
Website: www.mceducation.com

Distributed by
Oxford University Press
Great Clarendon Street, Oxford,
OX2 6DP, United Kingdom
www.oxfordprimary.co.uk
www.oxfordowl.co.uk

First published 2015
Reprinted 2015

ISBN 978-981-01-8862-7

Printed in the United Kingdom

Acknowledgements
Written by Dr Fong Ho Kheong, Chelvi Ramakrishnan and Bernice Lau Pui Wah

UK consultants: Carole Skinner, Simon d'Angelo and Elizabeth Gibbs

Cover artwork by Daron Parton

The authors and publisher would like to thank all schools and individuals who helped to trial and review Inspire Maths resources.